introductic

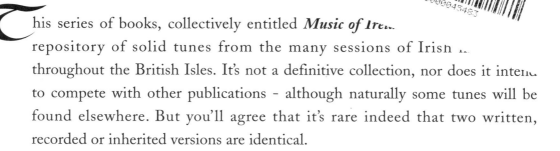

his series of books, collectively entitled *Music of Irel...* repository of solid tunes from the many sessions of Irish ... throughout the British Isles. It's not a definitive collection, nor does it inten... to compete with other publications - although naturally some tunes will be found elsewhere. But you'll agree that it's rare indeed that two written, recorded or inherited versions are identical.

Take each setting in this series as an individual; get the outline under your fingers and then make it your own, either through improvisation, by playing with other musicians, by investigating other manuscripts, by listening to good recordings, or, preferably, a combination of all of these. Never ever use a single source for your setting. Likewise, the harmony shown here is merely a launch pad. Most of the chords shown will fit most situations most of the time.

With this in mind, you'll notice that many alternative titles are included in the index. They help signpost the way around recordings and other books; they leaven the bread that is traditional music.

A tilde (~) above or below a note indicates where the tune might usually be embellished. If you have any questions or suggestions, please get in touch with the publishers at the address shown below.

David J Taylor
January 1997

Fire Away, Now!! first produced and published in England 1997 by Dave Mallinson Publications
3 East View, Moorside, Cleckheaton, West Yorkshire, England BD19 6LD
Telephone 01274 876388, *facsimile* 01274 865208, *e-mail* mally@mally.com, *web url* http://www.mally.com
ISBN 1 899512 31 4
British Library Cataloguing in Publication Data
A catalogue record for this book is available from the British Library
———————— ooOoo ————————
This series created by David J Taylor; all titles traditional except *Beverley Hill*, © Dave Hill amd used with permission
Harmony arrangements © David J Taylor 1996
Text set in *Caslon*; titling set in *Dorovar Carolus*; music engraved in *Interlude*; page layout in *Quark XPress*
Cover illustration © Karen Tweed 1995
First printed in England by RAP Limited, telephone 01706 44981
———————— ooOoo ————————

index

alternative titles are shown in *italics*

reels

doherty's reel

over the hill

king of the clans

the rambler in cork

dogs among the bushes

the jug of punch

the thrush in the storm

the bear island reel

the jolly seven

ballinasloe fair

the humours of westport

lucy campbell

the shaskeen

kiss me, kate

peg mcgrath

lads of laoise

johnny allen

the miller of droghan

beverley hill

buckley's fancy

the knocknaboul reel

the monaghan twig

the old torn petticoat

richard dwyer's no. 1

finbar dwyer's no. 3

the other high reel

the beauty spot

sweet biddy of ballyvourney

creamer's reel

paddy fahey's no. 6

john doherty's

the donegal

mcfadden's handsome daughter

man of the house

ryan's rant

jigs

kitty's wedding

maid on the green

the trip to killarney

up in the air

summer breezes

the kesh no. 2

trip to galway

paddy kelly's jig

mick gorman's jig

hornpipes

eleanor neary's hornpipe

the fairies' hornpipe

Lost in sligo Town

o'donnell's hornpipe

the perfect hornpipe no. 1

the perfect hornpipe no. 2

26

the peacock's feather no. 1

the peacock's feather no. 2

polkas

jack reedy's polka

G   G   Bm   C   D   G   Bm   C   D   G

Em   C   D   C   D   G   Bm   C   D   G

jim doyle's polka no. 1

G   Bm   D   G   G   Bm   D   D   G

G   Bm   D   D   G   C   G   D   G

tom sullivan's polka

D   D   D   A   G   D   E   A   C   A7   D

D   E   A   D   A   G   D   E   A   C   A7   D

D   E   A   D   G   A7   D   E   A   C   A7   D

the kerry rake

biddy martin's polka

terry teahan's polka no. 1

tourniore lasses

as i went out upon the ice

munster banks

the green cottage polka no. 3

freedom for ireland

cousins' delight

tureengarbh glen

johnny cope's polka

paddy kenny's polka

the four shoves no. 2